My First Holy Communion

PREPARING · CELEBRATING · REVIEWING · REMEMBERING

Text by
Frances C. Heerey, S.C.H.

Regina
Press

Nihil Obstat: Reverend Robert O. Morrissey, J.C.D.
                   Censor librorum
                   August 8, 2002

Imprimatur: Most Reverend William Murphy
                   Bishop of Rockville Centre
                   September 12, 2002

THE REGINA PRESS
10 Hub Drive
Melville, New York 11747

ISBN 0-88271-116-4
Printed in Hong Kong

Name _____

I was born on _____

I was baptized on _____

I received my First Holy Communion on

_____

Jesus answered and said to him, "Whoever loves me will keep my word, and my Father will love him, and we will come to him and make our dwelling in him"
                                                    John 14:23

Table of Contents

Preface

*When I found your words, I devoured them; they became
my joy and the happiness of my heart.*

Jeremiah 15:16

Dear Children and Parents,

To celebrate is to give honor to someone special. Our
First Holy Communion Day is the occasion when we
are honored to receive Jesus' Body and Blood. Jesus is
the Son of God. Jesus is the Word of God.

Jesus loved God and he loved people. It can be
imagined that he often went as a child to the market
place with his Mother Mary and his foster-father Joseph.
As an adult, he most likely spent time speaking with the
shoppers and store keepers. Jesus loved the people.

This is a celebration book. It is intended to bring Jesus
into the minds and hearts of children in a way that will
never be forgotten.

The text and illustrations are presented for children who
have been prepared to receive their First Holy
Communion and for those who have already celebrated
that momentous occasion. Here, in review, they can
meet Jesus, the Word of God, who entered their hearts in
joy and remains with them in sheer delight.

I Am Special

• *Preparing* •

God shared life with me through my parents. Life is a wonderful gift.

He calls me by my name

_____

because he loves me. I have goodness in me because he made me in his image and likeness. God calls me to use my special talents in the best way possible.

To live I need: food, clothing, shelter, love, peace. God calls me to help him care for the whole world and everything in it. He calls me to a spirit of justice and he wants me to have all I need.

• *Celebrating* •

Even before a word is on my tongue,
  LORD, you know it all.
Behind and before you encircle me
  and rest your hand upon me.
Such knowledge is beyond me,
  far too lofty for me to reach.

If I fly with the wings of dawn
  and alight beyond the sea,
Even there your hand will guide me,
  your right hand hold me fast.

You formed my inmost being;
  you knit me in my mother's womb.
I praise you, so wonderfully you made me;
  wonderful are your works!

Psalm 139:4-6, 9-10, 13-14

• *Reviewing and Remembering* •

1. *Why am I special?*
   I am special because I am made in the image and
   likeness of God.

2. *Who made me?*
   God made me through my parents.

3. *Why did God make me?*
   God made me because he loves me.

4. *What does God want me to do?*
   God wants me to love him. He wants me
   to love everybody.

5. *How do I show God that I love him?*
   I show God that I love him by praying to him,
   obeying his laws, helping him to care for the
   people and things of the earth.

6. *How do I express love for people?*
   I express love for people when I try to change
   things that are harmful for them. This is being a
   just person.

7. *What do all people need?*
   People have a need for food, clothing, shelter,
   love and peace.

8. *Do babies, old people, and handicapped people
   have needs?*
   Yes, they have a need for food, clothing, shelter,
   love and peace.

9. *Why are all people special?*
   All people are special because they are made in
   the image and likeness of God.

God
• *Preparing* •

God has a special name. We make a sign so that we can know God's Name.

In the name of the Father
and of the Son
and of the Holy Spirit.

Three persons in one God is called the

TRINITY

We can call God by name.
God created the world.
We can praise God.

Jesus is the Son of God.
The Holy Spirit is the spirit of Jesus.
The Holy Spirit gives us the power to live as
    children of God.

God is present among his people.
God shares his gifts of creation with us.
God cares for all living things.

• *Celebrating* •

The Lord is my shepherd
there is nothing I lack.
In green pastures you let me graze;
to safe waters you lead me;
you restore my strength.
You guide me along the right path
for the sake of your name.
Even when I walk through a dark valley,
I fear no harm for you are at my side;
your rod and staff give me courage.

Psalm 23:1-4

• *Reviewing and Remembering* •

1. *What are the names of the three persons in one God?*
   The names of the three persons in one God:
   God the Father, God the Son, God the
   Holy Spirit.

2. *What name do we give the divine mystery of
   three persons in one God?*
   We call the three persons in one God the
   Holy Trinity.

3. *What is the name of the Son of God?*
   Jesus is the Son of God.

4. *What work does the Holy Spirit do?*
   The Holy Spirit gives us the power to live as
   children of God.

5. *What prayer helps us remember the names of the*
   Trinity?
   The prayer is called "The Sign of the Cross."

6. *Where is God?*
   God is everywhere. God is especially present
   among his people.

7. *Who created the world?*
   God created the world out of nothing.

8. *What prayer can we say to honor God our Father?*
   We can pray the "Our Father."

9. *Who helps us to love God and to love each other?*
   The Holy Spirit helps us to love God and to love
   each other.

10. *What work does God do?*
    God cares for all living things. He cares for me.

11. *Why did God give us the gifts of the earth?*
    God gave us the gifts of the earth to make us
    happy and others happy.

Bible

• *Preparing* •

Stories tell us about people and events.

The BIBLE is the book all about God. It is also called Scripture or the Word of God. Reading the BIBLE is a good way to know who God is, and some of the things God has done for his people.

The BIBLE is divided into two main parts:
Old Testament and New Testament.

The Old Testament tells us how God loved his people before Jesus was born.

The New Testament tells us how God loved us so much that God gave us his Son, Jesus.

• *Celebrating* •

Keep your Bible in a special place in your home. This Word of God can be placed in the living room or in your bedroom. The BEST way to celebrate the Bible is to read from it and think about what God is saying to you in the scriptures.

Some holy words are taken and set to music. What holy songs or hymns do you like? Perhaps songs about Jesus or Mary are some of your favorites.

Here is a prayer to celebrate the Bible:
How I love your name, O Lord.
Your disciple John wrote down some of the scriptures.
His testimony is true, because he saw the things he wrote about Jesus.
I praise you, Jesus. Amen. Alleluia.

• *Reviewing and Remembering* •

1. *What is the Bible?*
   The Bible is a book which tells about God's word to God's people.

2. *What is another name used when people speak about the Bible?*
   They use the words "Sacred Scripture."

3. *Why did God give us the Bible?*
   God gave us the Bible so we can get to know God better.

4. *How is the Bible divided?*
   The Bible is divided into main books: the Old Testament and the New Testament.

5. *Where do we find Gospel stories about Jesus?*
   We find the gospel stories about Jesus in the New Testament.

6. *How can we respond to God's word?*
   We can respond to God's word in prayer and song, sharing it with other people, and by acting justly.

Jesus

• *Preparing* •

Jesus is the Son of God.

Jesus is our brother. We belong to him.

Jesus shows us how we can be good children of our heavenly Father. He teaches us how to pray. He teaches us how to act justly. He gives us the most wonderful gift of food which is himself in Holy Communion.

JESUS LOVES US VERY MUCH.

• *Celebrating* •

Oh, how I love you, Jesus!
My heart is bursting with LOVE for you.
You gave me your love,
And you showed me your life
And forever you take care of me!

Oh, how I thank you, Jesus.
My heart is bursting with THANKS to you.
You gave me my life
And you gave me my home
And forever I shall live with you.

Oh, how I praise you, Jesus.
My heart is bursting with PRAISE of you.
You gave me this world
And you gave me good friends.
And forever I shall PRAISE you,
Joyfully shouting:

I LOVE YOU, JESUS.

I THANK YOU, JESUS.

I PRAISE YOU, JESUS.

AMEN.

ALLELUIA.

• *Reviewing and Remembering* •

1. *Who is Jesus Christ?*
   Jesus is the Son of God, the second Person of the Blessed Trinity.

2. *Where was Jesus born?*
   Jesus was born in Bethlehem, about 2,000 years ago.

3. *Is Jesus God?*
   Jesus is God and he is also man.

4. *Who were the people who visited him when he was a baby?*
   The shepherds and the Magi from the east.

5. *Why did Jesus become Man?*
   Jesus became a man because he loves us and he wants to be with us. He wants to show us how to live.

6. *What are some of the things Jesus did?*
   a. He obeyed his mother Mary and his foster-father Joseph.
   b. He prayed to our heavenly Father.
   c. He took care of people who were in need.
   d. He gave peace to everyone.

7. *How can we be like Jesus?*
   We can be like Jesus by helping people in need, caring for babies, old people, and handicapped people. We must try to share what we have with people who have nothing.

8. *How is Jesus present to us today?*
   Jesus is present with his people in the Church, in the sacraments, especially in the Holy Eucharist.

9. *When did Jesus die?*
   Jesus died on Good Friday.

10. *Why do we celebrate Easter?*
    We celebrate Easter to honor Jesus' resurrection from the dead.

11. *Why do we celebrate Ascension Thursday?*
    We celebrate Ascension Thursday to honor the day that Jesus ascended into heaven to be with his heavenly Father.

12. *Will Jesus come again?*
    Yes, Jesus will come again on the last day; then he will judge the living and the dead.

God's Family

• *Preparing* •

Another name for God's Family is the Church. God loves God's family, the Church.

The Catholic Church is a community of people who praise and worship God, who care for one another, who celebrate the sacraments. Some people who take care of the Catholic Church are: Our Holy Father the Pope, Cardinals, Bishops, Priests, Deacons, Sisters, Brothers and other members of the laity.

To be good persons in the church, we must be good to all people. We are to let the light of our good deeds shine for all to see. We became members of the Church at our Baptism when our parents said "Yes." At that time the community, the church, welcomed us. They promised to help us know and love Jesus. This is done through certain signs called sacraments.

• *Celebrating* •

Let the prayer of Saint Francis of Assisi be a prayer
that I pray for the family, the church.

Lord, make me an instrument of your peace.
Where there is hatred, let me sow love;
where there is injury, pardon;
where there is doubt, faith;
where there is despair, hope;
where there is darkness, light;
where there is sadness, joy.

O Divine Master, grant that I may seek not so much
to be consoled as to console;
to be understood as to understand;
to be loved as to love;
for it is in giving that we receive;
it is in pardoning that we are pardoned;
and it is in dying that we are born to eternal life.
Amen.

• *Reviewing and Remembering* •

1. *What is the Catholic Church?*
   The church is God's family. The members of the
   church pray together, worship God, follow his
   Son Jesus, who started the Church, and care
   for one another.

2. *Who is the head of the Catholic Church?*
   Our Holy Father, the Pope, is the head of the
   Catholic Church.

3. *When did you become a member of the*
   Catholic Church?
   I became a member of the Catholic Church on
   the day I was baptized.

4. *What are the sacraments of the church?*

   There are seven sacraments:
   Baptism
   Confirmation
   Eucharist
   Penance
   Anointing of the Sick
   Holy Orders
   Matrimony

Baptism

• *Preparing* •

When we think of Baptism, we think of water.

Water is necessary for life. It supports our life and the life of plants and animals. We need it to drink and to cook our food. We use it to clean ourselves, our clothing, the things we use. Plants need it in order to grow. It is cool to drink when we are hot and thirsty. We swim in it for exercise and for fun. It helps to make us strong.

At Baptism, we were given a new life in God through water and the Holy Spirit. We were baptized in the name of the Father and of the Son and of the Holy Spirit. We were given power to praise God in prayer and worship. We were welcomed into God's family and we became followers of Jesus.

• *Celebrating* •

Peter [said] to them, "Repent and be baptized, every one of you, in the name of Jesus Christ for the forgiveness of your sins; and you will receive the gift of the Holy Spirit. For the promise is made to you and to your children and to all those far off, whomever the Lord our God will call."

Acts 2:38-40

Lord, I am glad that Saint Peter really listened to you when you told him how to help others become members of your church. I am happy that my parents had me baptized. I want to follow you all the days of my life, as a member of your church. Amen. Alleluia.

• *Reviewing and Remembering* •

1. *What is Baptism?*
   Baptism is a sacrament by which we become members of the Church, receive power to pray in Christian worship, and are born to a new, everlasting life by means of water and the Holy Spirit.

2. *How is Baptism given?*
   The priest, deacon, etc. baptizing pours water over the head of the person being baptized and says: "I baptize you in the name of the Father and of the Son and of the Holy Spirit."

3. *What does Baptism do?*
   Baptism gives the soul the indelible mark of a Christian; takes away original sin, all personal sin, and all punishment due to sin; it gives sanctifying grace.

Eucharist
• *Preparing* •

Some of our happiest times are when we share food with others at the kitchen or dining room table. We remember stories about other people and the good times that we have had. We thank people for what they have done and for what they are.

Jesus shared food with his people. Because he loved them, he shared bread and wine with his friends.

One particular evening, Jesus told his friends that the bread and wine were special. He told them he would make the bread and wine become his Body and Blood. Jesus read with his friends some stories that are in the Old Testament. The stories helped them remember good things God had done for God's people; that meal was called "The Last Supper."

Jesus' friends shared in the first celebration of the Eucharist that evening. They received the Body and Blood of Jesus. They received their First Holy Communion.

Eucharist means "thanksgiving." We remember to say "thanks" to God for giving us his Son Jesus in

Holy Communion. At Mass we remember that the cup contains the wine, the Blood of Jesus; that the bread is the Body of Jesus; that Jesus sanctified his life for us on the cross.

• *Celebrating* •

The best way to celebrate the Eucharist is to go to Mass. This is the way we celebrate Mass:

1. We sing our song of welcome:
    Penitential Rite

2. We ask forgiveness of our sins:
    Liturgy of the Word

3. We listen to God's Word as he speaks to us in the scriptures and in the homily:
    Liturgy of the Eucharist

4. We offer gifts of bread and wine. We offer ourselves to God.

5. We remember the words of Jesus at the Last Supper: Take this, all of you, and eat it:
    This is my Body which will be given up for you.
    Take this, all of you, and drink from it:
    This is the cup of my Blood, the blood of the new and everlasting covenant. It will be shed for you and for all so that sins may be forgiven.
    Do this in memory of me.

6. We receive Jesus in Holy Communion.

7. We thank and praise God our Father.

8. We receive the priest's blessing. He tells us to go out in PEACE to love and serve the Lord.

RESPOND TO JESUS

Jesus, my heart is filled with love for you. I thank you for the gift of yourself to me in Holy Communion. I know that you love me. I know that you care for me. I know that you give me courage and make me strong to do good things. I want to care for other people when they have needs, because you want me to care for them. Bless me, Jesus. Keep me close to you every day of my life, but especially today. Amen.

• *Reviewing and Remembering* •

1. *What is the Holy Sacrifice of the Mass?*
   The Holy Sacrifice of the Mass is the sacrifice of Jesus on the Cross.

2. *What happens at Mass?*
   At Mass Jesus changes bread and wine into his own Body and Blood through Sacred Scripture and the homily and the actions of the priest.

3. *What are the two main parts of the Mass?*
    The two main parts of the Mass are: the Liturgy of the Word and the Liturgy of the Eucharist.

4. *What do we remember at Mass?*
    We remember to praise God our Father.
    We remember that Jesus died for us.
    We remember that Jesus rose to a new life.
    We remember that Jesus sent us his Holy Spirit to be with us always.

5. *How do we receive Holy Communion?*
    We receive Holy Communion by walking reverently up to the minister of Communion (priest, deacon, or extraordinary minister). Either put out your tongue to receive Jesus, or place one hand on top of the other, receive the Host in your hand, and put it in your mouth.

6. *What should our hearts be like when we approach Jesus?*
    Our hearts should be loving hearts, for Jesus and for all other people.

7. *What special command does the priest give us at the end of Mass?*
    The priest tells us to "Go in Peace."

Sacrament of Penance

• *Preparing* •

Occasionally we find ourselves doing or thinking things that are hurtful to other people and to ourselves. Sometimes we do not do the things for others or ourselves that we are responsible for. When we do, think, or omit things on purpose, we disobey God's law of love. This is called sin. By sin we hurt others and ourselves.

How can we make up to God and to others? We can do that by being sorry and telling that to God and to others. We can tell God in the Sacrament of Reconciliation or Penance. We must remember the most important lesson learned: *God loves us very much!* God forgives us when we confess our sins to him.

At Confession we are welcomed back and we share PEACE with God and one another.

• *Celebrating* •

This is the way we celebrate the Sacrament of Penance in five steps.

BEFORE CONFESSION
1. We *think* of our sins, with Jesus.
2. We are *sorry* for our sins.
3. We *decide* not to sin again.

IN CONFESSION
The priest welcomes us.
We pray the Sign of the Cross.
The priest talks to us in the name of God, our Father.
He reads from the scriptures.

4. We *confess* what we did wrong. The priest helps us to do better. We tell God we are sorry. The priest forgives us in the name of God and God's people. He gives us a penance. We thank the priest and God.

AFTER CONFESSION
5. We do our penance.

A Simple Prayer

O God, I remember how wonderfully I am made.
You made me because you love me.
You made other people because you love them.
Sometimes I am not kind
    or I do not care for other people in need.
I know I have forgotten to love you and them.
I am really sorry.
I need you, Jesus,
    to help me love our Father and other people.
I need you, Father,
    to help me follow Jesus in his way of love.
I need you, Holy Spirit,
    to help me forgive and love other people
    who hurt me.

Thank you,
    for the gift of this wonderful sacrament
    which gives me the Peace of Jesus. Amen.

• *Reviewing and Remembering* •

1. *What is the Sacrament of Reconciliation or Penance?*
   Penance is the sacrament which gives us a special way to show God we are sorry for our sins. It is an action by which God shows his mercy and forgiveness.

2. *What is sin?*
   Sin is disobeying God's law of love deliberately.

3. *What is God's law of love?*
   God's law of love is found in the words of Jesus:

   This is the first:
   Hear, O Israel! The Lord our God is Lord alone!
      Therefore, you shall love the Lord your God
      with all your heart
      with all your soul
      with all your mind
      with all your strength

   This is the second:
   You shall love your neighbor as yourself.
                                          Mark 12:28

4. *What are the other Commandments that God has given us?*
God has given us the Ten Commandments.

5. *What is Confession?*
Confession is telling God that we have done certain sins and that we are sorry.

6. *How does the Church bring God's forgiveness in confession?*
The Church brings God's forgiveness in confession through the priest.

7. *What are the special steps we take in going to confession?*
    1. We think of our sins.
    2. We are sorry for our sins.
    3. We decide not to sin again.
    4. We confess what we did.
    5. We do our penance.

8. *What do we mean by "We do our penance"?*
Immediately after our confession, we say the prayers or do the activity that the priest gives us.

Mary

• *Preparing* •

When Jesus was a child, his Mother Mary taught him how to walk and to talk. She fed Jesus and made clothes for him. She taught him how to pray. Mary helped Jesus grow up to be a man.

Mary's life was a journey of faith to God. Mary was a very good person. She had respect for all life - plants, animals, and people. She helped take care of people when they were in need of care. She always obeyed God's Law of Love. Mary said "Yes" to God when he chose her to be the Mother of Jesus.

Because she is our mother too, Mary prays for us. It is good to ask Mary for help. She cares for us, the brothers and sisters of her Son.

A favorite prayer of people in God's family is the Hail Mary.

• *Celebrating* •

The rosary is a special way of praying to God that honors Mary, the Mother of Jesus. While reciting prayers, you think about certain stories in the lives of Jesus and Mary. These stories are called mysteries: a mystery is a story about God. The complete rosary consists of fifteen decades. There are four sets of mysteries and five stories in each set.

The Joyful Mysteries are:
Mondays and Saturdays

✝ **The Annunciation**
The Angel Gabriel tells Mary that she is to be the Mother of God.

✝ **The Visitation**
The Blessed Virgin pays a visit to her cousin Elizabeth.

✝ **The Birth of Jesus**
The Infant Jesus is born in a stable at Bethlehem.

✝ **The Presentation of the Child Jesus in the Temple**
The Blessed Virgin presents the Child Jesus to Simeon in the Temple.

✝ **The Finding of the Child Jesus in the Temple**
Jesus is lost for three days, and the Blessed Mother finds Him in the Temple.

The Mysteries of Light are:
Thursdays

✝ **The Baptism of Jesus**
Jesus is baptized in the Jordan River by
John the Baptist.

✝ **The Wedding at Cana**
Jesus attends a wedding at Cana in Galilee,
where he turns water into wine.

✝ **The Proclamation of the Kingdom of God**
Jesus goes through the towns and cities of his
own country proclaiming God's Kingdom
and helping the poor.

✝ **The Transfiguration**
Jesus leads his friends up a high mountain,
where they see him shining in glorious light.

✝ **The Institution of the Holy Eucharist**
At supper with his friends before he dies,
Jesus gives himself to them in bread and wine.

The Sorrowful Mysteries are:
Tuesdays and Fridays

✝ **The Agony of Jesus in the Garden**
Jesus prays in the Garden of Olives and drops of
blood break through His skin.

✝ **The Scourging at the Pillar**
Jesus is tied to a pillar and cruelly beaten
with whips.

† **The Crowning with Thorns**
A crown of thorns is placed upon Jesus' head.

† **The Carrying of the Cross**
Jesus is made to carry His cross to Calvary.

† **The Crucifixion**
Jesus is nailed to the cross, and dies for our sins.

The Glorious Mysteries are:
Wednesdays and Sundays

† **The Resurrection of Jesus from the Dead**
Jesus rises from the dead, three days after His death.

† **The Ascension of Jesus into Heaven**
Forty days after His death, Jesus ascends into heaven.

† **The Descent of the Holy Spirit**
Ten days after the Ascension, the Holy Spirit comes to the apostles and the Blessed Mother in the form of fiery tongues.

† **The Assumption of Mary into Heaven**
The Blessed Virgin is assumed into heaven.

† **The Crowning of Mary Queen of Heaven and Earth**
The Blessed Virgin is crowned Queen of Heaven and Earth by Jesus, her Son.

• *Reviewing and Remembering* •

1. *Who is Mary?*
    Mary is the Mother of Jesus and the Mother of God.

2. *Is Mary our Mother, too?*
    Yes, Mary is our Mother.

3. *What does Mary want us to do?*
    Mary wants us to follow her Son Jesus and to care for his people.

4. *What are some feasts we celebrate in Mary's honor?*
    Some feasts are: Annunciation, Immaculate Conception, Assumption.

5. *What is meant by the Immaculate Conception?*
    The Immaculate Conception means that Mary was free from original sin when she was born.

6. *What happened at the Annunciation?*
    The Annunciation celebrates the time when the angel Gabriel announced to Mary that she was chosen to be the Mother of Jesus.

7. *What is meant by the Assumption?*
    The Assumption means that when Mary died she was taken body and soul directly into heaven.

8. *Are there other feasts honoring Mary?*

Yes, these are all the feasts that honor Mary.

January 1:	Solemnity of Mary, the Mother of God
February 2:	Presentation of Jesus in the Temple
February 11:	Our Lady of Lourdes
March 25:	The Annunciation
May 31:	The Visitation The Immaculate Heart of Mary
July 16:	Our Lady of Mt. Carmel
August 5:	Dedication of St. Mary Major
August 15:	The Assumption of Our Lady
August 22:	The Queenship of Mary
September 8:	The Birth of Mary
September 15:	Our Lady of Sorrows
October 7:	Our Lady of the Rosary
November 21:	The Presentation of Mary
December 8:	The Immaculate Conception
December 12:	Our Lady of Guadalupe
December 25:	Christmas, the Birth of Our Lord

Prayer

Don't you like talking to your friends and listening to them when they tell you stories? Prayer is something like that. Prayer is talking to God. Prayer is listening to God. Prayer is just being with God.

Sometimes we pray alone (in our room, in church, anywhere). Sometimes we pray with others (family, friends, community). Sometimes we pray for others (sick, lonely, elderly, handicapped).

A good way to remember the kinds of prayer we pray is to think of the word ACTS. The letters stand for: ADORATION, CONTRITION, THANKSGIVING, SUPPLICATION.

A   Adoration - I adore you God, Father, Son, Holy Spirit.

C   Contrition - I confess my sins with real sorrow.

T   Thanksgiving - I thank you, God, for all your wonderful gifts.

S   Supplication - I ask you for special help for myself and others.

The church has also traditionally recognized a fifth type of prayer, PRAISE.

P   Praise - I praise you, God, for all my blessings.

Special Prayers That We Should Know
The Our Father

Our Father, who art in heaven, hallowed be thy name; thy kingdom come; thy will be done on earth as it is in heaven. Give us this day our daily bread; and forgive us our trespasses as we forgive those who trespass against us; and lead us not into temptation, but deliver us from evil. Amen.

The Hail Mary

Hail Mary, full of grace, the Lord is with thee. Blessed art thou among women, and blessed is the fruit of thy womb, Jesus. Holy Mary, Mother of God, pray for us sinners, now and at the hour of our death. Amen.

Glory Be to the Father

Glory be to the Father, and to the Son, and to the Holy Spirit. As it was in the beginning, is now and ever shall be, world without end. Amen.

Act of Contrition

My God, I am sorry for my sins with all my heart. In choosing to do wrong and failing to do good, I have sinned against you whom I should love above all things. I firmly intend, with your help, to do penance, to sin no more, and to avoid whatever leads me to sin. Our Savior Jesus Christ suffered and died for us. In his name, my God, have mercy.

The Apostles' Creed

I believe in God, the Father almighty, Creator of heaven and earth. I believe in Jesus Christ, his only Son, our Lord. He was conceived by the power of the Holy Spirit and born of the Virgin Mary. He suffered under Pontius Pilate, was crucified, died and was buried. He descended to the dead. On the third day he rose again. He ascended into heaven, and is seated at the right hand of the Father. He will come again to judge the living and the dead. I believe in the Holy Spirit, the holy Catholic Church, the communion of saints, the forgiveness of sins, the resurrection of the body, and life everlasting. Amen.

Grace Before Meals

Bless us, O Lord, and these your gifts which we are about to receive from your bounty, through Christ our Lord. Amen.

Grace After Meals

We give you thanks, almighty God, for these and all your blessings; you live and reign for ever and ever. Amen.

The Beatitudes

1. Blessed are the poor in spirit: the
   reign of God is theirs.

2. Blessed are the sorrowing: they shall
   be consoled.

3. Blessed are the lowly: they shall
   inherit the land.

4. Blessed are they who hunger and
   thirst or holiness: they shall have their fill.

5. Blessed are they who show mercy:
   mercy shall be theirs.

6. Blessed are the single-hearted: for
   they shall see God.

7. Blessed are the peacemakers: they
   shall be called sons of God.

8. Blessed are those persecuted for holiness'
   sake: the reign of God is theirs.

Works of Mercy

The Corporal Works of Mercy

To feed the hungry.

To give drink to the thirsty.

To clothe the naked.

To visit and ransom the captives.

To shelter the homeless.

To visit the sick.

To bury the dead.

The Spiritual Works of Mercy

To admonish sinners.

To instruct the ignorant.

To counsel the doubtful.

To comfort the sorrowful.

To bear wrongs patiently.

To forgive all injuries.

To pray for the living and the dead.

Commandments of God

The Ten Commandments of God

1. I, the Lord, am your God. You shall
   not have other gods besides me.
2. You shall not take the name of the Lord,
   your God, in vain.
3. Remember to keep holy the Sabbath Day.
4. Honor your father and your mother.
5. You shall not kill.
6. You shall not commit adultery.
7. You shall not steal.
8. You shall not bear false witness
   against your neighbor.
9. You shall not covet your neighbor's wife.
10. You shall not covet anything that belongs
    to your neighbor.

The Precepts of the Church

1. To keep holy the day of the Lord's resurrection.
2. To receive Holy Communion frequently
   and the Sacrament of Reconciliation regularly.
3. To study Catholic teaching.
4. To observe the marriage laws of the Church.
5. To strengthen and support the Church.
6. To do penance.
7. To join in the missionary spirit of the Church.

Stations of the Cross

This is a prayer said during Lent. Many people say it all year round. There are fifteen stations.

Prayer

Jesus, I want to be sorry for my sins. Help me to see how you suffered and died for me. Help me to know your mercy and forgiveness, Teach me how to say, "Thank You."

1. JESUS IS CONDEMNED TO DIE
   I am sorry, Jesus.

2. JESUS CARRIES HIS CROSS
   It looks so heavy, Jesus.

3. JESUS FALLS FOR THE FIRST TIME
   Your strength is starting to fail.

4. JESUS MEETS HIS MOTHER MARY
   How sad your Mother felt, Jesus.

5. SIMON HELPS JESUS
   I must help others who carry heavy loads.

†

6. VERONICA WIPES JESUS' FACE
   Teach me to help others in need.

†

7. JESUS FALLS A SECOND TIME
   Dear Jesus, how weak you are.

†

8. JESUS MEETS THE WOMEN
   Jesus, you're so brave. You tell them not to cry.

†

9. JESUS FALLS THE THIRD TIME
   Dear Jesus, you are suffering so much.

†

10. JESUS IS STRIPPED OF HIS CLOTHES
    How shamefully you were treated.

†

11. JESUS IS NAILED TO THE CROSS
    How cruel the people were. I love you.

†

12. JESUS DIES
    I know you forgive me my sins.

13. JESUS IS TAKEN DOWN
I thank the people who took care of your body.

14. JESUS IS LAID IN THE TOMB
Thank you for your mercy.

15. JESUS RISES FROM THE DEAD
I rejoice with you, Jesus.

Seasons of the Church Year

The family of God likes to celebrate God all year round during the seasons of the church year. The seasons are: Advent, Christmas, Lent, Easter, Pentecost, Ordinary Time.

Advent

This is a time in which the community prepares for the celebration of Jesus' birthday. Advent is a happy time when we awaken our hearts by praying special prayers or by having an advent wreath or by burning a Mary candle.

Advent celebration is about four weeks long.

Christmas

Christmas is the time when we celebrate the birthday of Jesus. It is a time of gift-giving to others. Giving gifts reminds us of the best gift of all which our Father in heaven gave to us: Jesus our Brother.

During the Christmas season we remember Mary the Mother of God, the Holy Family, the Epiphany when the Magi visited Jesus. We celebrate Jesus as the Prince of Peace.

Lent

Lent is the time in which the community prepares for the celebration of the death and resurrection of Jesus. It is a serious time when we look at Jesus' great care and love for us. We do penance for our sins and tell Jesus and each other "I am sorry, please forgive me."

Jesus forgives us through his suffering and death on the Cross.

During Lent we get ready for the new life and joy of Easter.

Easter

Easter is the most wonderful time when we celebrate the resurrection of Jesus. God raised Jesus from the dead. It is a time of great joy. It is the alleluia time!

Jesus brings new life to the world. Every Sunday we celebrate the feast of the Lord's resurrection.

Pentecost

Forty days after Jesus was raised from the dead, he ascended into heaven where he is seated at the right hand of the Father.

Afterwards, his Mother Mary and the disciples waited in prayer for the coming of the Holy Spirit. On the day of Pentecost they had all gathered together in one place. The Holy Spirit appeared before the Apostles in tongues of fire. He sent them out to preach to the whole world the good news of Jesus. He told them to proclaim that all who believe and are baptized shall be saved.

Ordinary Time

This is the rest of the time during the year when we worship God, by celebrating the Resurrection of Jesus and by listening to stories about the life and teachings of Jesus.

Jesus said,

"I WILL BE WITH YOU ALL DAYS,
EVEN UNTIL THE END OF TIME."